The Christmas Kit

Published by Prim-Ed Publishing

www.prim-ed.com

Foreword

The Christmas Kit contains activities from across the curriculum, including English, mathematics, science, geography, R.E., art and design technology.

The package enables pupils to work independently, in small groups or as a whole class under teacher direction. It has been designed to capture the pupil's imagination and promote creativity while addressing skill development and cross-curricular learning.

Activities include:

- comprehending the meaning of Christmas;
- exploring Christmas traditions around the world;
- following directions in making Christmas gifts and cards;
- reading and performing plays;
- text analysis;
- letter/diary writing; and
- problem solving.

Comprehensive teachers notes for each page, including learning objectives to explain the learning focus of the activity, background information, answers and additional activities, have been included to save precious time at this stage of the year.

Merry Christmas and have fun!

Titles in this series are:
The Christmas Kit – Lower
The Christmas Kit – Middle
The Christmas Kit – Upper

Contents

Teacher Notes ii
Assessment Proforma iii

Developmental Activities
Finger Puppets .... 2 – 3
Angel Crackers .... 4 – 5
Christmas Countdown .... 6 – 7
Christmas Bells .... 8 – 9
Stained Glass Star Shower .... 10 – 11
Nativity Shadow Puppets .... 12 – 13
Christmas Gift Tags .... 14 – 15
Santa's Clever Elves .... 16 – 17

Christmas Gifts
Concertina Christmas Card .... 18 – 19
Merry Photo Frame .... 20 – 21
Angel Promise .... 22 – 23
Christmas Lights .... 24 – 25

Christmas Play
The First Christmas Tree .... 26 – 29

What is Christmas?
The Story of Christmas .... 30 – 33
Christmas Around the World – 1 .... 34 – 35
Christmas Around the World – 2 .... 36 – 37

Christmas Contract
Christmas Toy Hunt .... 38 – 39
Who Has the Presents? .... 40 – 41
Get Ready for Christmas! .... 42 – 43
Sort Santa's Sack .... 44 – 45
Ho! Ho! Hold on! .... 46 – 47
Spot the Differences .... 48 – 49
Letter to Santa .... 50 – 51
Christmas Colouring .... 52 – 53
Santa's Christmas Clues .... 54 – 55
Colour and Count .... 56 – 57
Rudolph's Jigsaw .... 58 – 59
Star Magic .... 60 – 61

Teachers Notes

Each pupil page is supported by a teacher's page which provides the teacher with the following information.

- *Learning objectives* guide the teacher as to the behaviours that pupils should be demonstrating through completing the activity.
- *Materials* are clearly listed to aid in the quick preparation of activities. All resources can be gathered beforehand to aid in the smooth running of the lesson.
- *Background information* has been provided where necessary to give the teacher any additional information that may be needed. This information could be the history behind the topic covered on the pupil page, a point of interest or an additional resource that may be useful.
- *Additional activities* have been suggested as a way to extend pupils or to further develop the ideas on the pupil page.
- *Answers* have been provided where necessary for easy marking of the pupil worksheet.

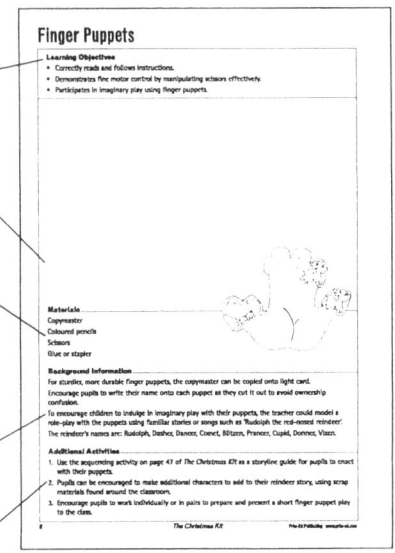

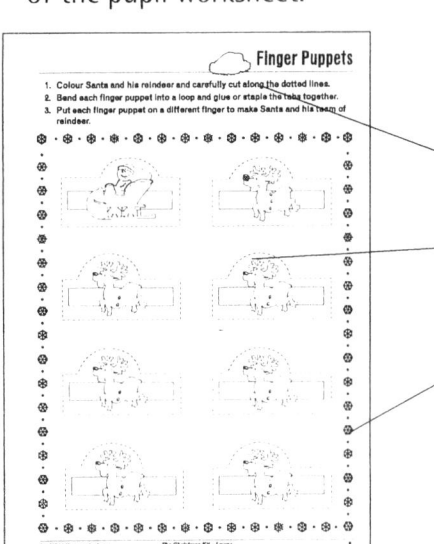

- *Instructions* are clear and easy for pupils to follow. They have been written to suit the specific age group.
- *Activities* provide opportunities for pupils to demonstrate skills and knowledge gained over the school year.
- *Artwork* complements the activity and has been drawn to suit the age of the pupils.

Using the Assessment Proforma

Fill in the appropriate learning area.

Give a brief description of the activities in the chosen copymaster and what was expected of the pupils.

List the learning objectives(s) assessed on the chosen copymaster.

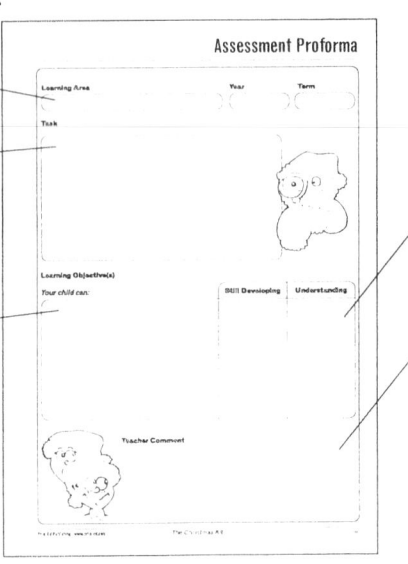

Complete the continuums to indicate pupil progress.

Use this space to comment on an individual pupil's performance which cannot be indicated in the formal assessment, such as work habits or particular needs or abilities.

The Christmas Kit — Prim-Ed Publishing www.prim-ed.com

Assessment Proforma

Learning Area

Year

Term

Task

Learning Objective(s)

Your child can:

	Still Developing	Understanding

Teacher Comment

_____
_____
_____
_____

Finger Puppets

Learning Objectives
- Correctly reads and follows instructions.
- Demonstrates fine motor control by manipulating scissors effectively.
- Participates in imaginary play using finger puppets.

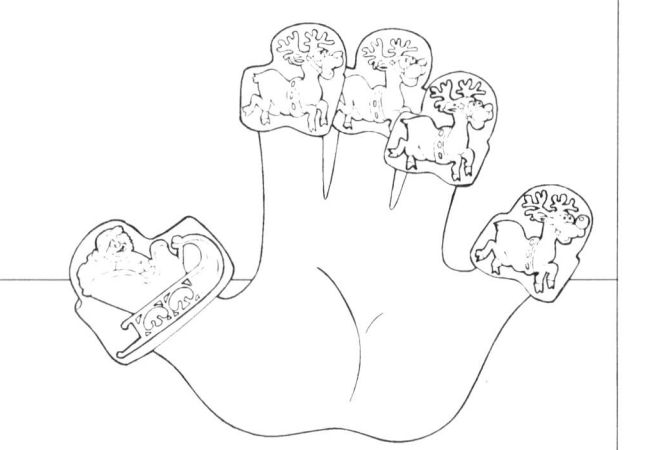

Materials

Copymaster

Coloured pencils

Scissors

Glue or stapler

Background Information

For sturdier, more durable finger puppets, the copymaster can be copied onto light card.

Encourage pupils to write their name onto each puppet as they cut it out to avoid ownership confusion.

To encourage children to indulge in imaginary play with their puppets, the teacher could model a role-play with the puppets using familiar stories or songs such as 'Rudolph the red-nosed reindeer'.

The reindeer's names are: Rudolph, Dasher, Dancer, Comet, Blitzen, Prancer, Cupid, Donner, Vixen.

Additional Activities

1. Use the sequencing activity on page 47 of *The Christmas Kit* as a storyline guide for pupils to enact with their puppets.
2. Pupils can be encouraged to make additional characters to add to their reindeer story, using scrap materials found around the classroom.
3. Encourage pupils to work individually or in pairs to prepare and present a short finger puppet play to the class.

Finger Puppets

1. Colour Santa and his reindeer and carefully cut along the dotted lines.
2. Bend each finger puppet into a loop and glue or staple the tabs together.
3. Put each finger puppet on a different finger to make Santa and his team of reindeer.

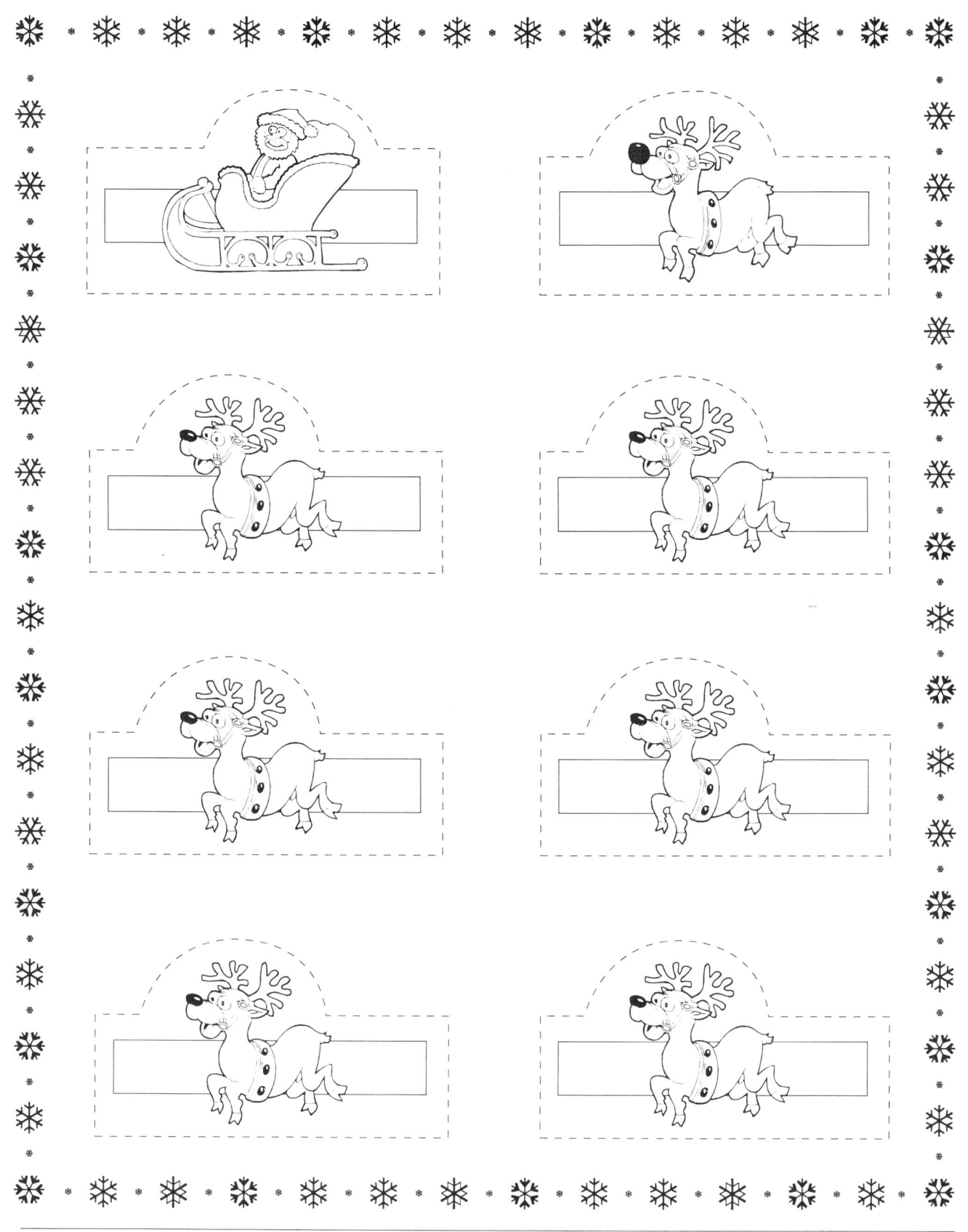

Angel Crackers

Learning Objectives
- Correctly reads and follows instructions.
- Demonstrates fine motor control by manipulating scissors effectively.
- Can write a joke suitable for a Christmas cracker.

Materials

Copymaster
Pencils
Glue or sticky tape
Crepe paper
Curling ribbon
Scissors

Background Information

Christmas crackers are a tradition for many families on Christmas Day. They are pulled at the dinner table during Christmas lunch.

Crackers are best made as a small-group project, with a helper such as a parent or older pupil who is able to assist with tying ribbon and following instructions.

Crackers for the crackers are available at craft shops and may be included if desired. Similarly, sweets, or small gifts such as cheap jewellery, can also be put inside the cracker.

When complete, the pupils could be encouraged to use their cracker as a gift for a family member or friend.

Additional Activities

1. Should the pupils choose to give their crackers as a gift, the gift tags on page 15 of *The Christmas Kit* could be used to label them.
2. Discuss where the tradition of using crackers began. Make a list of other traditional events which take place in the pupils' households on Christmas day. Be sensitive to the different ways in which each family chooses to celebrate and encourage the pupils to appreciate the diversity within their class.

Angel Crackers

You will need:
- 1 toilet tissue tube
- Crepe paper
- 2 pieces of ribbon
- Coloured pencils
- Glue

What to do:
1. Colour the angel and the cracker wrapping using bright colours and cut along the dotted lines.
2. Write a joke on the special 'joke' tag and cut along the dotted lines.
3. Cover your toilet tissue tube with crepe paper and tie one end with ribbon.
4. Place the joke inside the cracker and tie the other end with ribbon.
5. Glue the cracker wrapping around the cracker.
6. Glue the angel onto the wrapping, leaving the wings unstuck. This will make your angel stand out better.

Joke

Christmas Countdown

Learning Objectives
- Demonstrates fine motor control by manipulating small objects effectively.
- Reads numbers and count backwards from 24.

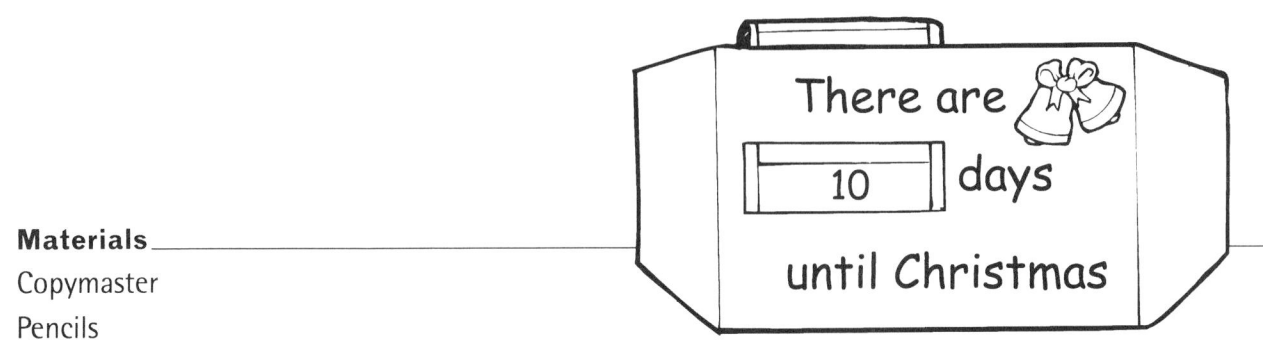

Materials
Copymaster
Pencils
Toothpicks
Lolly sticks
Drinking straw
Sticky tape
Glue

Instructions for Making the Christmas Countdown
1. Colour as desired and cut along dotted lines.
2. Fold back along black lines on the frame.
3. Join the number strips together by overlapping and gluing along the tag.
4. When dry, roll the number strips tightly around a pencil to curl.
5. Thread the number strips through the slots in the countdown frame with numbers facing forward.
6. Attach each end of the number strips to a lolly stick or plastic straw, allowing the stick or straw to 'hang out' on one side as a winder.
7. Roll the number strip tightly starting at the '1' end and leaving the number '24' showing through the slot.
8. Use the lolly stick or plastic straw winders to 'roll' through to the next number each day.

Background Information

The Christmas countdown can be constructed and placed on each pupil's desk from the first of December. Each day, the pupils can roll the calendar down to the next number and read how many days are left until Christmas. The Christmas countdown could be used in conjunction with a class Advent calendar with the traditional significance of each day discussed with the pupils.

According to the Christian faith, Advent is a time of preparation, waiting and hope over the four weeks before Christmas. Among the customs of Advent, the Advent wreath is probably the most important. Lighting the Advent candles each day with a prayer can prepare your household for Christmas. For pupils, marking off the days before Christmas with an Advent calendar can be an aid for living the season.

Additional Activities
1. Use 'The Twelve Days of Christmas' as inspiration for creating a class book based on counting backwards.
2. Compare the numbers decreasing on the countdown calendar to the numbers increasing on an Advent calendar. Discuss why they are different.

Christmas Countdown

Carefully cut along the dotted lines.

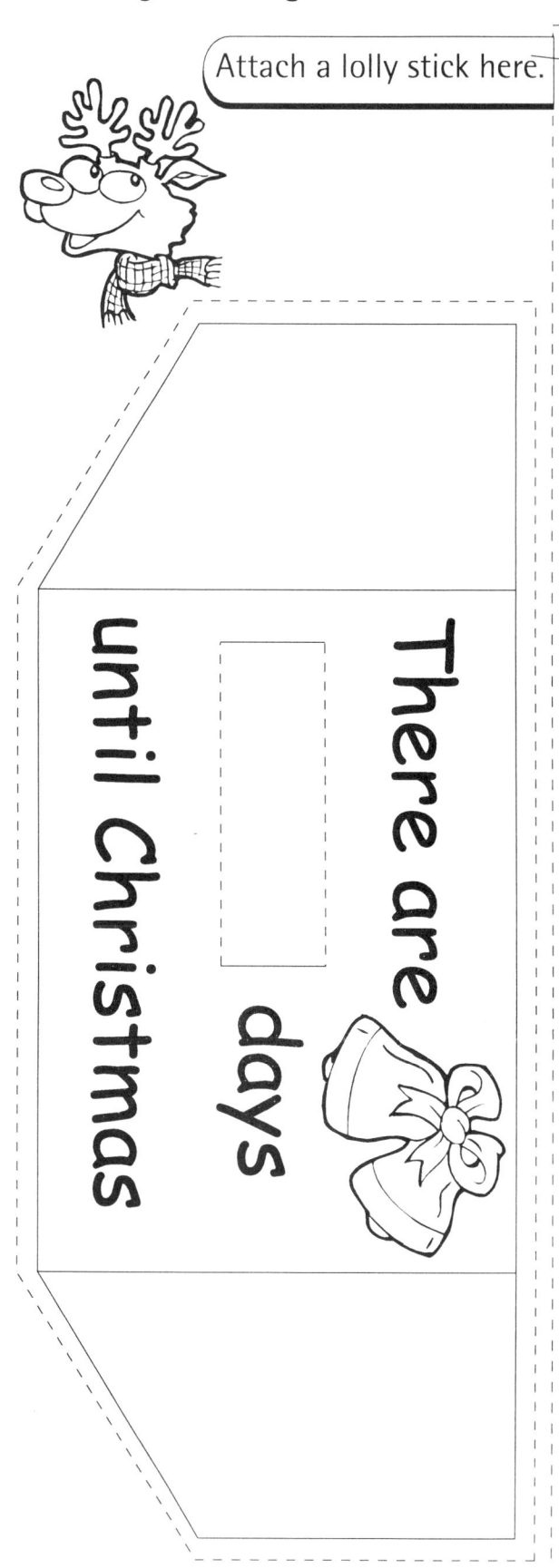

Attach a lolly stick here.

There are ___ days until Christmas

1	13
2	14
3	15
4	16
5	17
6	18
7	19
8	20
9	21
10	22
11	23
12	24

Attach a lolly stick here.

Christmas Bells

Learning Objectives
- Correctly reads and follows instructions.
- Demonstrates fine motor control by manipulating small objects effectively.

Materials

Copymaster

Coloured pencils

Curling ribbon or string

Glue or sticky tape

Background Information

The original purpose of bells was to make a loud, but not necessarily musical, sound to drive off evil spirits. For this reason, bells are rung during festivals and processions, including Christmas. Today, church bells are sounded on Christmas Day to announce the beginning of a worship service.

Additional Activities

1. Pupils can be encouraged to create their own paper decorations such as paper chains or simple shapes cut from paper or card, with curling ribbon or string used to hang them on a class tree.
2. Discuss the reasons why bells are associated with Christmas.
3. Investigate other materials which could be used to make Christmas bell decorations. Encourage the pupils to test their construction theories and share how they made their bells with the class.

Christmas Bells

1. Colour the patterns on each bell and carefully cut out.
2. Bend each bell into a cone shape and glue or staple the tab on the inside of the bell.
3. Thread a piece of string or ribbon through the point of each bell, leaving a knot on the inside.

Stained Glass Star Shower

Learning Objectives
- Correctly reads and follows instructions.
- Selects appropriate colours for a stained glass window.

Materials

Copymaster

Wax crayons

Cooking oil

Kitchen paper

Background Information

Stained glass windows are most effectively displayed on windows in full sun. The luminous quality of stained glass windows traditionally represents the 'Light of the Lord' and has been used in churches and places of worship for centuries.

Additional Activities

A stained glass window effect can also be achieved by:
1. Cutting and gluing coloured paper onto black paper or card in a mosaic fashion.
2. Gluing overlapping cellophane of different colours onto cling wrap and carefully cutting the dried product into Christmas shapes or frames.
3. Placing coloured cellophane or tissue paper between sheets of greaseproof paper and ironing together to melt the wax and create a sheet which can be cut into Christmas shapes or framed.

Stained Glass Star Shower

1. Colour the 'star shower' using wax crayons.
2. Cut around the border of the picture.
3. Dip in oil and drain on kitchen paper.
4. Stick picture against a window while still damp with oil.

Nativity Shadow Puppets

Learning Objectives
- Correctly reads and follows instructions.
- Demonstrates fine motor control by manipulating scissors effectively.
- Participates in imaginary play using shadow puppets.
- Recounts a familiar story.

Materials

Copymaster

Scissors

Toothpicks

Sticky tape

Overhead projector and screen

Background Information

For sturdier, more durable shadow puppets, the copymaster can be copied onto light card.

Encourage pupils to write their name onto each puppet as they cut it out to avoid ownership confusion.

To encourage pupils to indulge in imaginary play with their puppets, the teacher could model a role-play of the nativity story with the puppets.

The Nativity Story

The story of Christmas is thought to have originated from the Gospels of Saint Luke and Saint Matthew in the New Testament. According to the Gospel of Saint Luke, an angel appeared outside the town of Bethlehem to some shepherds and told them of the birth of Jesus. The Gospel of Saint Matthew tells how the Wise Men (kings) followed a bright star which led them to Jesus.

The first mention of Christmas in the Roman calendar occurred in AD 336; 25 December was indicated as a day of observance. By 1100, Christmas had become the most important celebration in Europe. During the 1400s and 1500s, artists such as Botticelli and Sandro painted scenes of the nativity. These paintings depict Jesus in the manger with Mary, Joseph, the shepherds, farm animals and the Wise Men (kings).

Additional Activities

1. Activities about the Nativity story can be found on pages 30 – 33 of *The Christmas Kit*. The pupils should be encouraged to discuss the beliefs and traditions held by their families to explore ways in which we are all different and special.
2. Introduce or expand a dress-up corner to include costumes relating to the Nativity or other traditional Christmas-related stories.
3. Enhance shadow puppet plays by using cellophane to create a colourful background or make a particular object stand out.

Nativity Shadow Puppets

1. Carefully cut around each shape.
2. Use sticky tape to attach a toothpick to the back of each shape.
3. Use the toothpicks as handles to move the shapes across an overhead projector glass to act out the Nativity story.

Christmas Gift Tags

Learning Objectives

- Correctly reads and follows instructions.
- Demonstrates fine motor control by manipulating scissors effectively.
- Uses festive colours appropriate to Christmas gift tags.

Materials

Copymaster

Pencils

Scissors

Background Information

Gift tags can be made available for pupils to use as they create various Christmas gifts for their families and friends. Pages 20 – 25 of *The Christmas Kit* include simple gift ideas to which the tags could be attached.

Alternatively, the gift tags could be produced as part of a small-group or whole-class activity to be taken home and attached to gifts.

To add extra 'sparkle' to the gift tags, allow pupils to experiment with using paints, crayons, glitter, cellophane and other materials from around the classroom.

Additional Activities

1. Hold a class 'secret Santa' using the tags made in class to identify whether a gift is for a boy or a girl. Be sure to set a maximum price to be spent on the gift and buy a couple of extra gifts yourself for those pupils who forget or are unable to bring a gift.
2. Encourage pupils to design their own gift tags using a range of materials from around the classroom.

The Christmas Kit

Christmas Gift Tags

1. Colour each gift tag and cut carefully along the dotted lines.
2. Fold in half to make small cards to put on Christmas presents.

Santa's Clever Elves

Learning Objectives
- Listens carefully and understands what has been asked.
- Uses a series of clues to identify an unknown object.

Materials

Copymaster

Pencils

Background Information

Barrier games are designed to improve oral language and are ideal for pupils in lower primary who are either new to using English or slow to develop pragmatic skills. Barrier games force pupils to verbalise questions which address specific aspects of a picture or situation, or require the use of positional or directional language. Barrier games are also an excellent means of promoting good listening comprehension skills in a fun, non-threatening manner.

Suggestions for Using 'Santa's Clever Elves'

1. Copy the stimulus picture 'The Clever Elves' onto an overhead transparency. Ask questions to encourage pupils to use listening comprehension skills; e.g. How many balloons are in the room with the Christmas tree? Alternatively, children could take turns answering 'yes' or 'no' to questions from other class members to determine a mystery object or person; e.g. Is it an elf? Is he carrying something?
2. Give pupils directions using positional language to determine a specific location or to make a path through the stimulus picture.
3. Play 'clue' games, such as 'Who am I?' or 'What am I?'. Pupils can take turns to give clues about a mystery object or person they have chosen.
4. Use the stimulus picture in pairs or small groups, taking turns to give directions, ask questions, or give clues.

Additional Activities

1. Brainstorm the activities happening in the picture to develop a pool of Christmas words for the pupils to include in their own writing.
2. Make dioramas of Santa's workshop in pairs or small groups using found objects. Be sure the pupils make a plan of how their diorama will be constructed and the materials they will need before they begin.

Santa's Clever Elves

The Christmas Kit

Concertina Christmas Card

Learning Objectives
- Correctly reads and follows instructions.
- Writes a short message appropriate for a Christmas card.

Materials

Copymaster

Pencils

Scissors

Background Information

The Christmas card was invented by British innovator Sir Henry Cole in 1843. He commissioned a well-known artist, J.C. Horsely, to design the picture for the card. Horsely adopted the common medieval artistic form of a triptych (three sets of illustrations). The central piece depicted a jolly party of adults and children with plenty of food and drink. Underneath this picture was expressed the seasonal greeting, wishing 'a merry Christmas and a happy New Year to you'. Each of the two side panels was a representation of good works—the clothing of the naked and the feeding of the hungry.

Additional Activities

1. Make Christmas decorations that require the children to create concertinas. For example, fold coloured paper in a tight concertina and tie string firmly around the middle of the strip. Fan each side of the paper to create 'wings', which could be attached to a dove or angel construction that is simply decorated with glitter or ribbon and hung on the Christmas tree.

2. Encourage children to design and make their own 'concertina' card, thinking carefully about how the card will open and what kinds of pictures will be appropriate.

Concertina Christmas Card

1. Colour Santa and his reindeer and carefully cut along the dotted lines.
2. Bend the card along the lines to make a 'concertina'.
3. Write a message to someone who is special to you inside the card.

Merry Christmas

Fold out

Fold in

Prim-Ed Publishing www.prim-ed.com *The Christmas Kit*

Merry Photo Frame

Learning Objectives
- Correctly reads and follows instructions.
- Demonstrates fine motor control by manipulating scissors effectively.

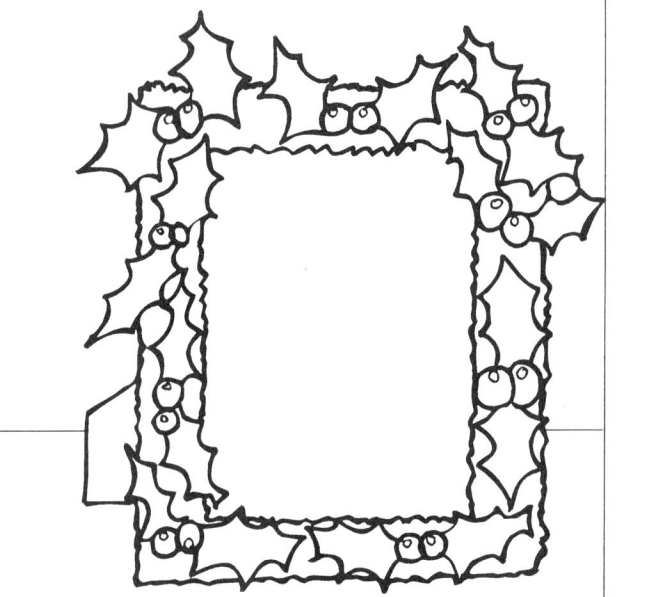

Materials

Copymaster copied onto card

Pencils

Scissors

Red crepe paper

Background Information

To ensure the frame will support the weight of its decorations and a photo, use medium weight cardboard or glue the back half or the frame to heavy card before cutting the support stand. If heavy card is used, a teacher or helper will need to cut the support stand with a blade.

The tradition of using holly originated when the early church banned the use of mistletoe in Christmas celebrations because of its pagan origins. Holly was believed it to be an appropriate substitute for Christmas greenery. Mistletoe had been used some 200 years before the birth of Christ by the Druids, to celebrate the coming of winter. The Druids believed the plant had special healing powers, while Scandinavians thought of mistletoe as a plant of peace and harmony. They also associated mistletoe with their goddess of love, Frigga. It is from this association that the custom of kissing under the mistletoe probably derived.

Additional Activities

1. Discuss the types of photos which the pupils might put in their photo frame to stimulate discussion on different types of families and the ways they choose to celebrate Christmas.
2. Put photos of each class member in the frames and create a class photo album for display. These photos can then be archived in a 'big book' and put in the school library. The pupils will love to look back on their photos as they progress through the school.
3. Discuss the reason why holly is used to represent Christmas. Investigate how the climate during December is different in different parts of the world. (See pages 34 – 35.)

Merry Photo Frame

1. Colour the holly leaves and carefully cut along all dotted lines.
2. Glue holly leaves and scrunched up pieces of red crepe paper onto the front part of the frame to make holly.
3. Glue three sides of the front part of the frame to the back of the frame.

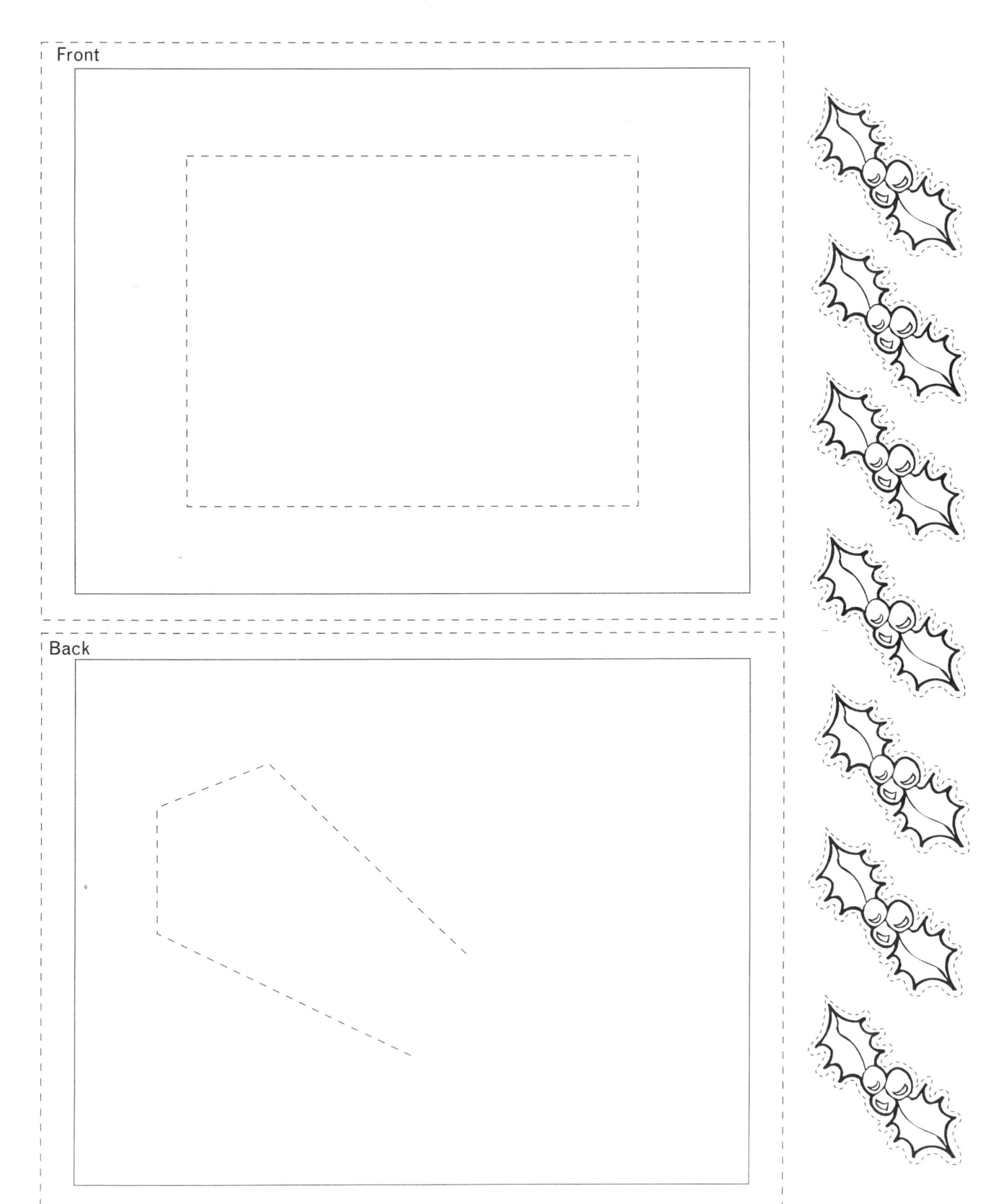

Front

Back

Angel Promise

Learning Objectives
- Writes a 'promise' which is appropriate as an 'I owe you' gift.

Materials

Copymaster

Coloured pencils

Scissors

Ribbon if desired

Background Information

An 'I owe you' is an inexpensive but effective way for pupils to join in 'giving' at Christmas and encourages them to value and experience the joy of giving, rather than focusing on receiving.

When the copymaster is completed, it can be cut out and rolled into a scroll. This may be fastened with ribbon if available or perhaps a Christmas sticker.

Additional Activities

1. Discuss and list gifts which do not cost money. Have the pupils focus on giving gifts such as these on a regular basis or in response to good deeds others have done for them.

Angel Promise

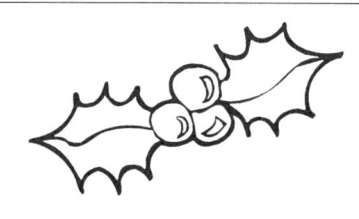

Dear _____

I made this little promise,

Full of Christmas cheer.

I promise to

_____

_____

And I'm going to keep it,

on the day I've written here!

Love from

_____

Christmas Lights

Learning Objectives
- Follows written and verbal directions to 'cook' Christmas lights.
- Reviews the purpose of creating Christmas lights.
- Evaluates the success of his or her cooking effort.

Materials

Copymaster

$^2/_3$ cup of sugar

1 cup of water

food colouring

toothpicks or curling ribbon

Pencils

Baking tray

Greaseproof paper

Instructions for Making 'Christmas Lights'

1. Boil sugar and water in a saucepan until it forms a thick syrup.
2. Grease a baking tray or line a tray with greaseproof paper.
3. Add food colouring to the syrup.
4. Spoon syrup onto the tray to make sweets about the size of a 20p piece. Press toothpicks into the setting mixture to make handles. Alternatively, the ends of a ribbon can be pressed into the cooling mixture to make a loop which can be used to hang the Christmas light sweets as an ornament.
5. Cool in the fridge overnight

If desired, sprinkles of the children's choice can be added before the 'Christmas lights' are placed in the fridge.

Safety tips
- Pupils should only be allowed to add food colouring and stir the boiling mixture with assistance from an adult.
- Mixture must be spooned onto trays by an adult. (Pupils can complete the first part of the activity sheet while this is happening.)
- Pupils should add decorative sprinkles after the mixture has cooled slightly on the tray.

Please note: To avoid burns, do not leave the children alone with hot items at any time.

Additional Activities

1. Hang 'Christmas lights' on a class Christmas tree or use as decorations around the classroom.
2. Wrap 'Christmas lights' in cellophane and tie with curling ribbon as a gift for family or friends.

Christmas Lights

'Christmas lights' are sweets you can use to decorate your Christmas tree or as gifts for your family and friends.

To make 'Christmas lights' you will need:
- sugar
- water
- food colouring
- toothpicks or curling ribbon

What to do!
1. Boil sugar and water.
2. Add food colouring.
3. Spoon onto the ends of toothpicks or ribbons. You will need to let your 'Christmas lights' cool in the fridge overnight!

Answer the questions in the boxes.

1. Tick a box.
- I used toothpicks. ☐
- I used ribbon. ☐
- I used toothpicks and ribbons. ☐

2. Tick a box.
- I will hang my 'Christmas lights' on the Christmas tree. ☐
- I will give my 'Christmas lights' away as presents. ☐

3. How happy were you with the way your 'Christmas lights' looked?

4. How did they taste?

The First Christmas Tree

Learning Objectives
- Reads and understands a playscript.
- Performs a character in a play.

Background Information

The playscript is based on the legend of the first Christmas tree. It has been written to involve every child in the class—as a main character, minor character or as part of the chorus. This will depend on the confidence and ability level of the pupils in your class.

The play could be performed in front of the following audiences:
- one or two other classes
- parents and relatives of the class
- whole-school Christmas concert

Suggested stage floor plan

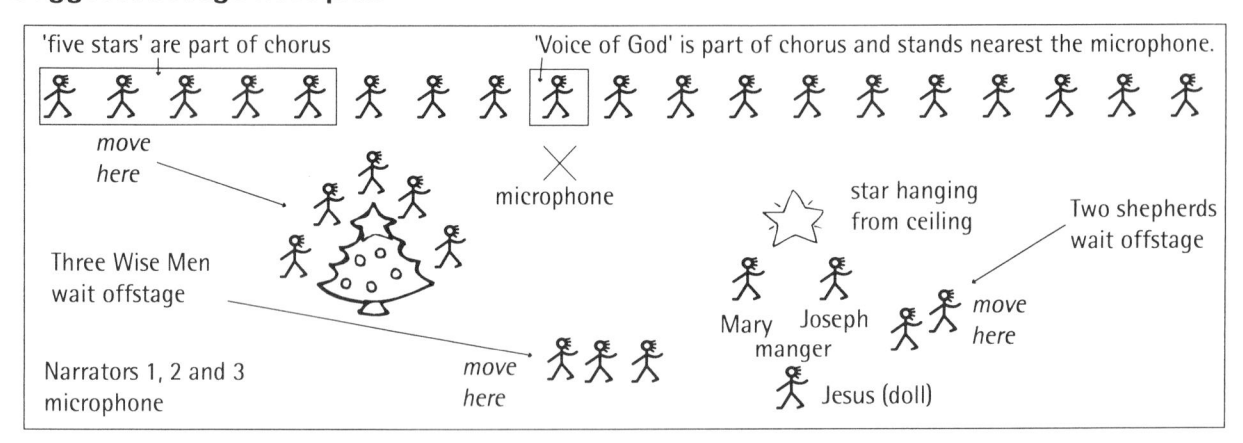

'five stars' are part of chorus

'Voice of God' is part of chorus and stands nearest the microphone.

move here

microphone

star hanging from ceiling

Two shepherds wait offstage

Three Wise Men wait offstage

Mary Joseph
manger

move here

Narrators 1, 2 and 3 microphone

move here

Jesus (doll)

Props

Do not need to be elaborate.

Suggestions:

Manger –	Wooden box; cardboard box painted brown
Straw –	Shredded paper
Animals –	Toy sheep, oxen, donkey; cardboard cut-outs; simple masks and blankets for children to be animals
Guiding star –	Silver-covered cardboard star hung from ceiling
Gifts –	Frankincense (fancy bottle), Myrrh (velvet-covered box), gold (jewellery or gold-covered 'ingot')
Candles –	A small torch with yellow or red cellophane over the lens.

Costumes

Mary –	Blue robe, or sheet over shoulder and tied around the middle with a sash. Shawl over head. Sandals.
Joseph –	Brown robe, or sheet over shoulder and tied with a rope or sash. Teatowel over head with headband. Sandals.
Shepherds –	As for Joseph, but different subdued colours or stripes. Crook for each.
Three Wise Men	Brightly coloured robe or sheet. Cummerbund around waist. Crown made of cardboard and glitter.
Five stars and chorus –	White sheet over shoulders. White, gold or silver sash. White socks. Star mask for face. Cut triangles from light card and staple around the outside of a paper plate. Cut away inside circle for the child's face. Attach elastic.
Narrators –	Dressed as shepherds (without a crook) or dressed as angels with a white sheet and halo.

The First Christmas Tree

Characters:
Joseph
Mary
baby Jesus
Three Wise Men
two shepherds
the Christmas Tree
five stars
chorus
three narrators
the voice of God

Setting:
Stable interior, night. Joseph and Mary stand behind the baby Jesus in the manger; left centre stage is a small fir tree (the first Christmas tree)

NARRATOR:	The baby Jesus had been born to Mary and Joseph. Many came to offer Him gifts. The first were the shepherds.
ALL (including chorus offstage):	(Sing first verse of 'While Shepherds Watched Their Flocks by Night' as shepherds enter, bearing gifts.)
SHEPHERDS:	We are just poor shepherds, but we offer these gifts to the baby Jesus. (Place gifts at foot of manger; step to one side.)
NARRATOR 2:	Then the ancient kings were next. These Three Wise Men had followed a heavenly star to the stable.
ALL (including chorus offstage):	(Sing first verse of 'We Three Kings" as wise men enter, bearing gifts.)
FIRST WISE MAN:	For this holy baby I bring a gift of frankincense. (Places gift on floor)

The First Christmas Tree

Before you start
- Before beginning rehearsals make the pupils familiar with the story of the First Christmas Tree.
- Get pupils to close their eyes and imagine what it would have been like on the night the story took place.
- Discuss what it would have felt like, looked like and smelt like.
- Identify with the characters.

When you practice
- While rehearsing the play get the children to visualise where they are to move and how they are to move. For example: How would each Wise Man walk?
- Practise the movements without words to encourage the pupils to use their bodies to create the character.
- Practise speaking roles without the chorus first.
- Practise songs separately first.

Christmas Carols

'Oh Christmas Tree' (Traditional)

O Christmas tree, O Christmas tree,
Thou tree most fair and lovely.
O Christmas tree, O Christmas tree,
Thou tree most fair and lovely.
The sight of thee at Christmas-tide
Spreads hope and gladness far and wide.
O Christmas tree, O Christmas tree,
Thou tree most fair and lovely.

Silent Night (Traditional)

Silent night, holy night!
All is calm, all is bright.
Round yon Virgin, Mother and Child.
Holy infant so tender and mild,
Sleep in heavenly peace,
Sleep in heavenly peace.

We Three Kings of Orient (Public Domain)

We three kings of Orient are,
Bearing gifts we traverse afar,
Field and fountain, moor and mountain,
Following yonder Star.
Chorus
O, star of wonder, star of might,
Star with royal beauty bright,
Westward leading, still proceeding,
Guide us to the perfect light.

While Shepherds Watched Their Flocks (Public Domain)

While Shepherds watch their flocks by night
All seated on the ground
The angel of the Lord came down
And glory shone around
'Fear not', said he for mighty dread
had seized their troubled mind
'Glad tidings of great joy I bring
To you and all mankind'

The First Christmas Tree

SECOND WISE MAN:	Holy infant, please accept my gift of gold. (Places gift on floor)
NARRATOR 3:	The little fir tree in the stable was unhappy. She wanted to give the infant Jesus a gift, too, but had nothing to give.
CHRISTMAS TREE:	All I have to offer Him are my pine needles, but they will surely prick His hand and hurt Him. I wish I had something to give Him.
NARRATOR 1:	And the little Christmas tree hung her head in shame.
NARRATOR 2:	But God in Heaven had heard the little tree's sad words, and He whispered to the stars.
GOD:	Go down to the earth, and rest on the branch of the little tree who wishes to offer a gift to the baby Jesus.
ALL:	(Sing first verse and chorus of 'Oh, Christmas Tree' as 'stars' enter, carrying lighted 'candles' which they hold beside and above the Christmas tree.)
NARRATOR 3:	The Christ child looked up at the lights and smiled. And the little Christmas tree was the happiest tree in the world.
NARRATOR 1:	And to this day, people put lights on their Christmas tree to remind them of that joyous event.
ALL (including chorus offstage):	(Sing 'Silent Night' as stage darkens except for stars on Christmas tree.)

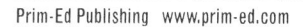

The Story of Christmas

Learning Objectives
- Reads and understands the story of Christmas.

Materials

Copymaster

Background Information

The story of Christmas is thought to have originated from the Gospels of Saint Luke and Saint Matthew in the New Testament. According to the Gospel of Saint Luke, an angel appeared outside the town of Bethlehem to some shepherds and told them of the birth of Jesus. The Gospel of Saint Matthew tells how the Wise Men (kings) followed a bright star which led them to Jesus.

The first mention of Christmas in the Roman calendar occurred in AD 336; 25 December was indicated as a day of observance. By 1100, Christmas had become the most important celebration in Europe. During the 1400s and 1500, artists such as Botticelli and Sandro painted scenes of the Nativity. These paintings depict Jesus in the manger with Mary, Joseph, the shepherds, farm animals and the Wise Men (kings).

Additional Activities

1. Use a corrector pen to delete appropriate words from the text and make a cloze. Complete in small groups or as a class using an overhead projector. Alternatively, laminate the sheet so pupils can individually complete the answers with a semipermanent felt pen.
2. Isolate phrases in Christmas carols to point out the significance of the words relating to the story of Christmas. For example, *Silent Night*, *Away in a Manger* and *We Three Kings*.

The Story of Christmas

Long ago, in a town called Nazareth, there lived a carpenter called Joseph. He was to marry a young woman by the name of Mary.

One night, Mary had a dream. In her dream, an angel sent by God told her she was going to have a baby. The baby would be the Son of God. Mary was to call him Jesus. She was very pleased that she had been chosen to be the mother of God's son. Mary told Joseph about the dream.

Later that year, a special census was called by the ruler of the land. This meant everyone had to return to the place where they were born so their names could be recorded. Mary and Joseph had to travel to the town of Bethlehem. It was a long way to Bethlehem. As Mary was due to give birth soon, she rode on the back of a donkey. Joseph walked next to her.

At last they reached Bethlehem. Joseph and Mary stopped at several inns to ask for a room. All the rooms were full. At last, one kind innkeeper let them use his stable. Joseph cleaned the stable and lined a feed trough with fresh straw to use as a bed. That night, the baby Jesus was born. The manger became His crib.

A bright star shone above Bethlehem after Jesus was born. Some shepherds in the fields were told by an angel to follow the star that would lead them to the baby Jesus.

Three kings in the east also saw the star and knew what it meant. They followed the star to the stable and arrived with gifts for Jesus. One brought a gift of frankincense, one a gift of myrrh and the other a gift of gold. The kings returned to the east to tell everyone about the birth of Jesus.

The Story of Christmas

Learning Objectives
- Extracts information to answer questions about the story of Christmas.
- Completes word study activities using vocabulary from the text.

Materials
- Copymaster
- Coloured pencils
- Dictionary (optional)

Additional Activities
1. Pupils write a different comprehension question from the story and swap with a friend.
2. Make a list of five words from the story and learn how to spell them, put them in alphabetical order and write each in a sentence.

Answers
1. (a) inn (b) manger (c) stable (d) census
2. (a) Jesus (b) Mary (c) Joseph (d) angel (e) king (f) shepherd (g) innkeeper
3. Teacher check
4. They were born in Bethlehem and had to return there for the census.
5. All the rooms were full in every inn.

The Story of Christmas

Answer the questions.

1. **Write a word from the story to complete each sentence.**

    (a) An _____ is a small hotel for travellers.

    (b) A _____ is a box from which cattle or horses eat.

    (c) A _____ is a place where horses are kept and fed.

    (d) A _____ is the counting of all the people who live in a place or country.

2. **Use the letters a, e, i, o or u to complete the names of these people in the story.**

    (a) J___s___s   (b) M___ry   (c) J___s___ph

    (d) ___ng___l   (e) k___ng   (f) sh___ph___rd

    (g) ___nk___ ___p___r

3. **Use your own words to tell what the angel said to Mary.**

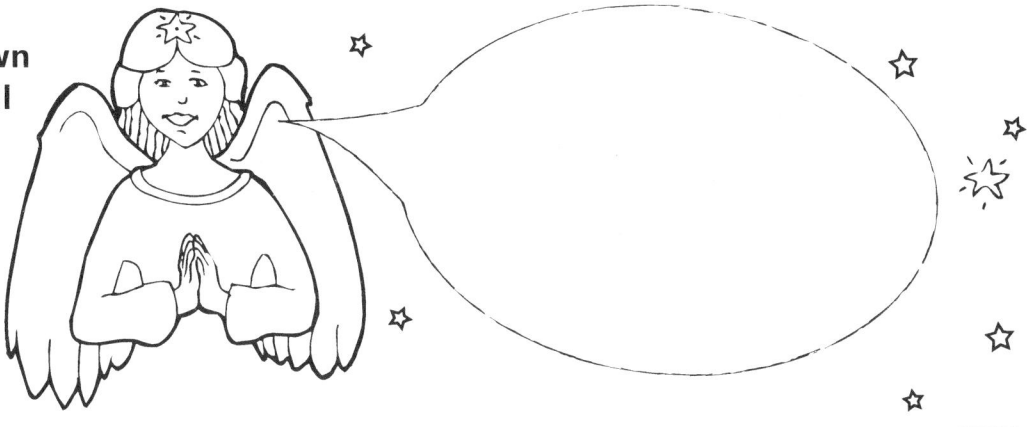

4. **Why did Mary and Joseph have to travel to Bethlehem?**

    _____

    _____

5. **Why did they stay in a stable?**

    _____

    _____

Christmas Around the World – 1

Learning Objectives

- Reads and understands.
- Describes the weather at Christmas time in the pupil's locality.
- Realises the weather at Christmas is different throughout the world.
- Learns of countries experiencing winter or summer at Christmas.
- Sorts clothing pictures into winter and summer clothes.

Materials

- Copymaster
- Coloured pencils/felt pens
- Scissors
- Glue
- World map

Background information

While some regions in the world do not experience four distinct seasons (generally the equatorial areas), Christmas for many falls in either winter—the northern hemisphere, or summer—the southern hemisphere.

Teachers could display a map of the world and assist pupils to locate the countries mentioned on the map. The map would also enable pupils to comprehend the 'northern' and 'southern' hemispheres.

Additional activities

1. Pupils could brainstorm words and phrases into winter and summer Christmas concepts. For example: Australia, England, snow, heat, go for a swim, keep warm, have a barbecue, make a snowman, beach, sled.
2. Pupils could investigate the types of foods eaten at Christmas in various places. Does the weather change the choice?

Answers

1. Teacher check
2. (a) Winter clothes – boots, scarf, gloves, jacket, jumper, umbrella, hat
   (b) Summer clothes – sun hat, sandals, T-shirt, shorts, swimming costume

Christmas Around the World – 1

1. **Christmas Day falls on 25 December.** What is the weather like where you live at that time of year? _____

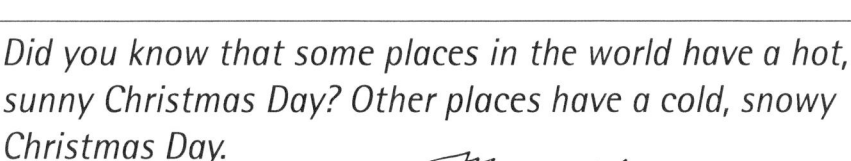

   Did you know that some places in the world have a hot, sunny Christmas Day? Other places have a cold, snowy Christmas Day.

   In countries such as England, Holland and Sweden, Christmas Day is during winter.

   In countries such as Australia, New Zealand and South Africa, Christmas Day is during summer.

2. **Sort the clothes below.**
   (a) Draw a blue circle around the clothes a child would wear in England at Christmas time.
   (b) Draw a red circle around those for Australia.

Christmas Around the World – 2

Learning Objectives
- Attempts to say 'Merry Christmas' in different languages.
- Completes cloze activities to read about some Christmas traditions in other countries.
- Uses word study skills to complete words about Christmas traditions.

Materials

Copymaster
Coloured pencils
World map

Background information

Use a map of the world and assist pupils to locate each of the countries mentioned in the activities.

Parents, relatives or friends of pupils who have or still follow different Christmas traditions could be invited to talk to the class and share experiences.

Additional activities

1. Ask pupils to share how to say and write 'Merry Christmas' in any languages they use at home.
2. Construct a class graph of the Christmas traditions listed in activity 3. Others could also be added.

Answers

1. Ireland – Nollaig Shona Dhuit
   Spain – Feliz Navidad
   Korea – Sung Tan Chuk Ha
   Germany – Froehliche Weihnacten
2. (a) Belgium, December, bread, Jesus
   (b) Finland, fir, dinner, casseroles
3. (a) stocking   (b) plum pudding   (c) wreath   (d) tinsel
   (e) crackers   (f) mistletoe   (g) turkey   (h) Christmas tree

Christmas Around the World – 2

1. **Match each country to its Christmas greeting. The words all say 'Merry Christmas'. Colour each pair of bonbons the same.**

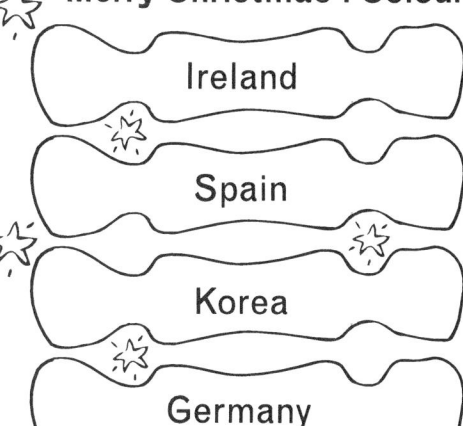

   Ireland — Sung Tan Chuk Ha
   Spain — Froehliche Weihnacten
   Korea — Nollaig Shona Dhuit
   Germany — Feliz Navidad

2. **Fill in the missing words to read about some Christmas traditions.**

   (a) In _____, children receive their gifts from 'Saint Nicholas' on 6 _____. Small family gifts are given at Christmas too. A special sweet _____ in the shape of baby _____ is eaten on Christmas morning.

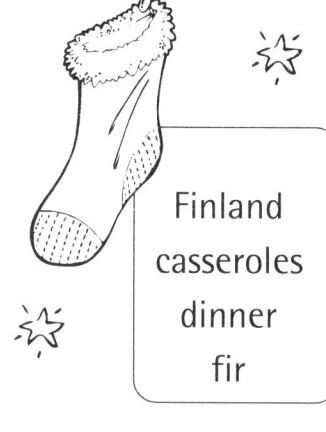

   bread, Belgium, December, Jesus

   (b) In _____, families decorate a _____ tree on Christmas Eve. Later in the day a special Christmas _____ is eaten. It includes little _____ with macaroni and vegetables.

   Finland, casseroles, dinner, fir

3. **The words below are all Christmas traditions. Use the letters a, e, i, o or u to finish each word. Circle it if you follow that tradition in your house.**

   (a) st__ck__ng
   (b) pl__m p__dd__ng
   (c) wr__ __th
   (d) t__ns__l
   (e) cr__ck__rs
   (f) m__stl__t__ __
   (g) t__rk__y
   (h) Chr__stm__s tr__ __

Christmas Toy Hunt

Learning Objectives
- Uses problem-solving strategies to solve a logic grid.

Materials

Copymaster

Coloured pencils

Background Information

Depending on the individual pupil's development, some will need more assistance than others to complete this activity. Ensure pupils can read any difficult words before attempting the activity.

The activity could also be completed in pairs or small groups with a supervisor.

Additional Activities

1. Pupils could make up another elf's name and a missing toy and hiding spot with clues to guess. Swap with a classmate or read out to the class.
2. Role-play the elves realising the toys are missing and each elf's search for his/her toy.

Answers

Holly – pram – bedroom

Tinsel – ball – lounge

Bauble – bicycle – stable

Ivy – teddy bear – kitchen

Christmas Toy Hunt

Holly, Ivy, Tinsel and Bauble are elves who are very cross. Merry, who is a mischievous elf, has hidden the toys each of the elves had finished making. The four elves must search for the missing toys.

Use the clues to find out the toy each elf made and where it was found. Draw the toy in the correct room below.

Bauble made a toy with two wheels you can ride on. He found it where the reindeer shelter.

Tinsel made a toy you can kick in the garden. He found it in a room where you would find a settee.

Holly made a toy that a doll could be pushed around in. She found it in a room you can sleep in.

Ivy made a furry toy you can cuddle. She found it in a room where you cook.

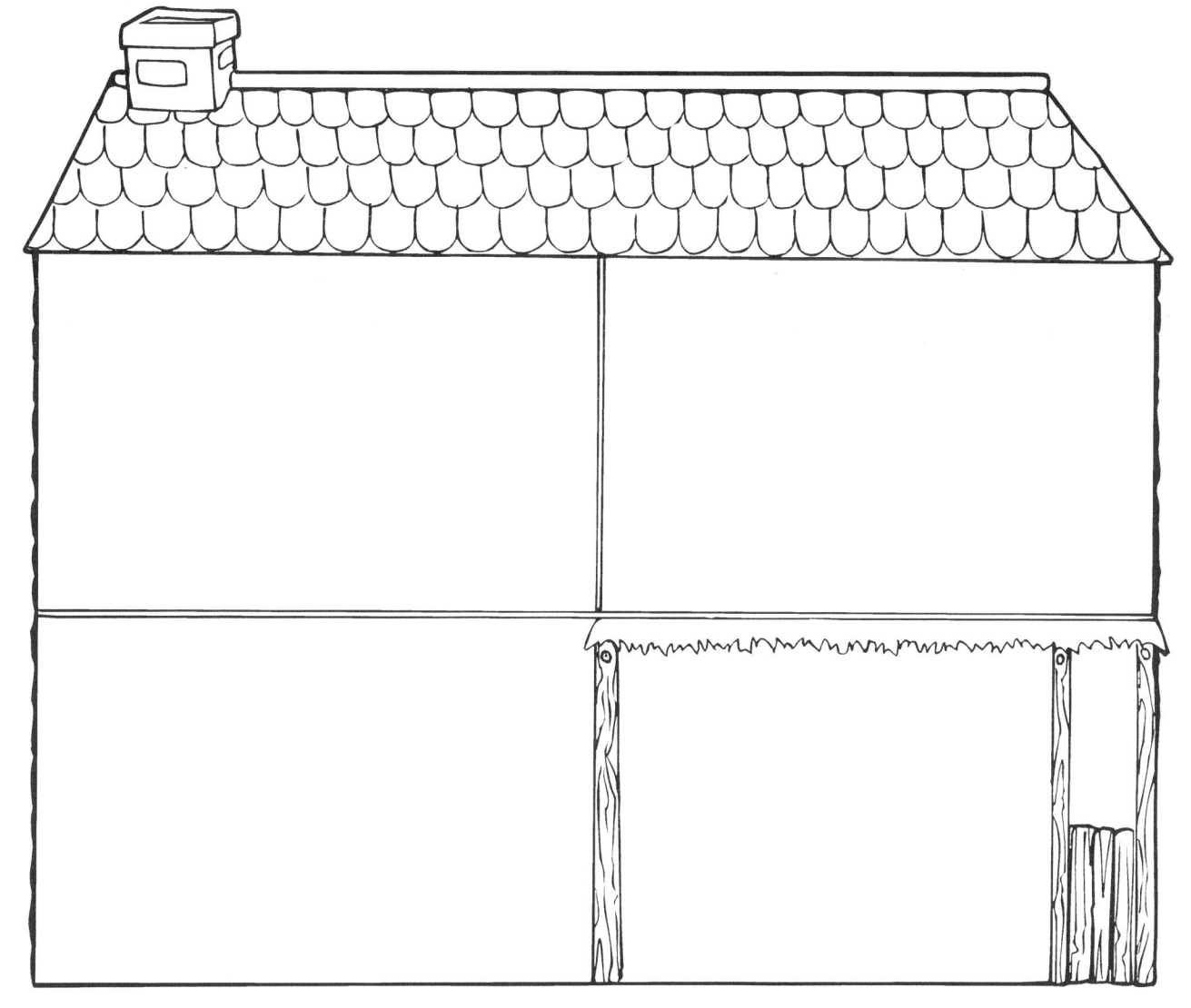

Who Has the Presents?

Learning Objectives
- Read and comprehend a simple text.
- Make innovations to a text based on prior knowledge of Christmas traditions.

Materials

Copymaster

Coloured pencils

Scissors

Background Information

This eight-page book has been designed to encourage young readers to use their imagination, predict possible solutions to the missing part of a text and use picture clues to derive the most appropriate sentence ending. The format allows pupils to take their book home and read it repeatedly, thus reinforcing new words in keeping with the Christmas theme, such as 'reindeer', 'Santa', 'Mrs Claus', 'elves' and 'presents'.

Instructions

1. Cut along all dotted lines.
2. Fold along all solid lines.
3. Fold in half lengthways.
4. Holding the ends, push middle pages outwards to form an eight-page booklet.

Additional Activities

1. Use the finger puppets on page 2 of *The Christmas Kit* to act out the story.
2. Create a class 'big book' based on the theme 'Who Has the Presents?', using the pupils in the class as characters and allowing them to choose what they were doing.
3. Have a Christmas 'treasure hunt' to find the 'missing presents'. Use positional language to give the pupils clues as to their whereabouts.

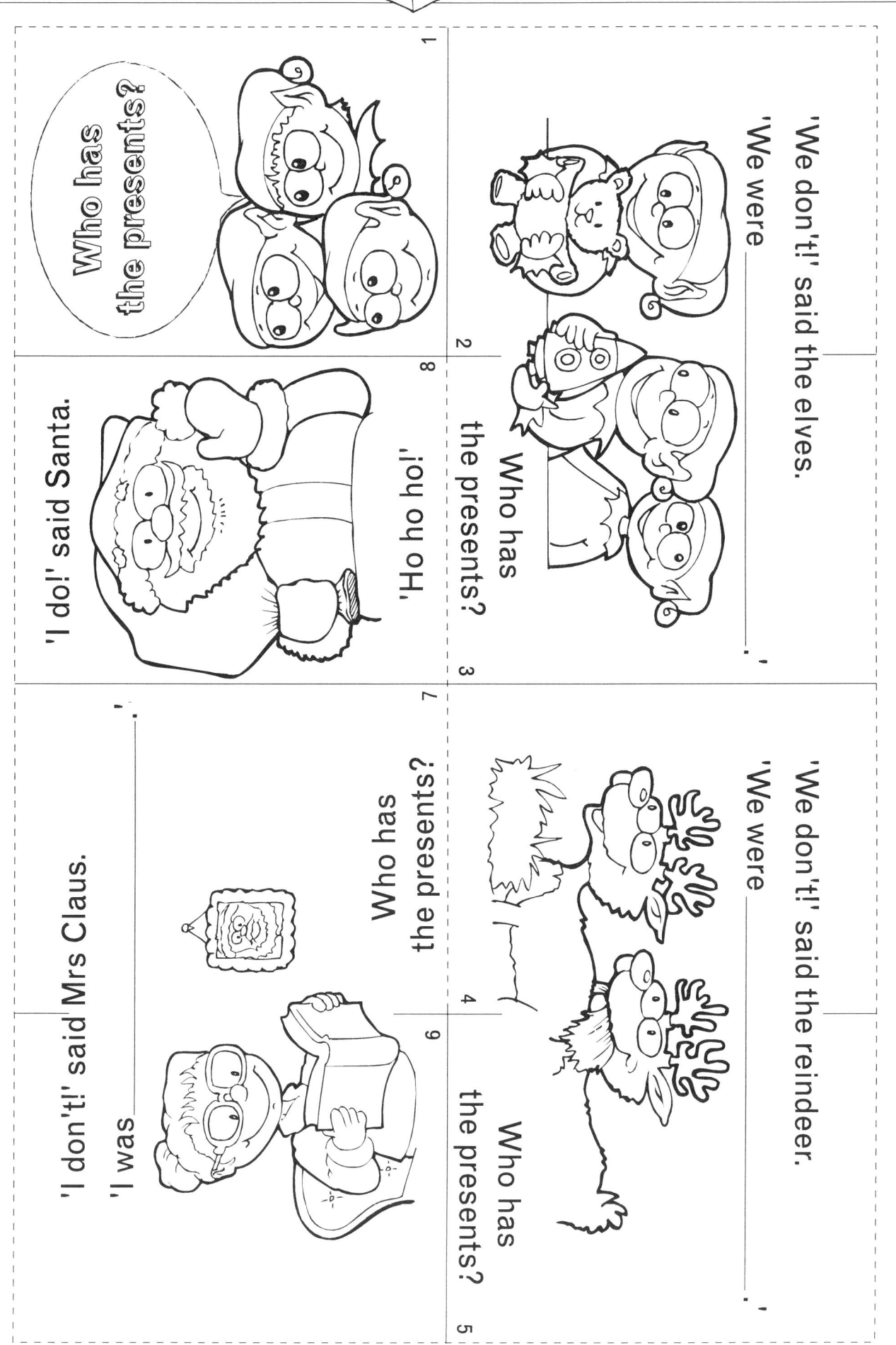

Who Has the Presents?

'We don't!' said the elves.
'We were _____.'

"Who has the presents?"

'We don't!' said the reindeer.
'We were _____.'

Who has the presents?

Who has the presents?

Who has the presents?

Who has the presents?

'Ho ho ho!'

'I do!' said Santa.

'I don't!' said Mrs Claus.
'I was _____.'

Get Ready for Christmas!

Learning Objectives

- Recalls the activities associated with Christmas in their family.
- Completes activities investigating events which occur before, during and after Christmas Day.

Materials

- Copymaster
- Coloured pencils

Additional Activities

1. Develop a class time line in the form of a wall story depicting the events occurring around Christmas.
2. Develop a class 'to do' list to organise activities prior to Christmas.
3. Discuss things which can be re-used or recycled at Christmas. Make Christmas cards using pictures cut from old Christmas cards or make decorations such as paper chains from old Christmas paper.

Answers

1. Answers will vary
2. Answers will vary
3. Wrapping paper, decorations and the pictures from Christmas cards can be recycled.

Get Ready for Christmas!

1. What do you do to get ready for Christmas? Colour the decorations which describe the things you do.

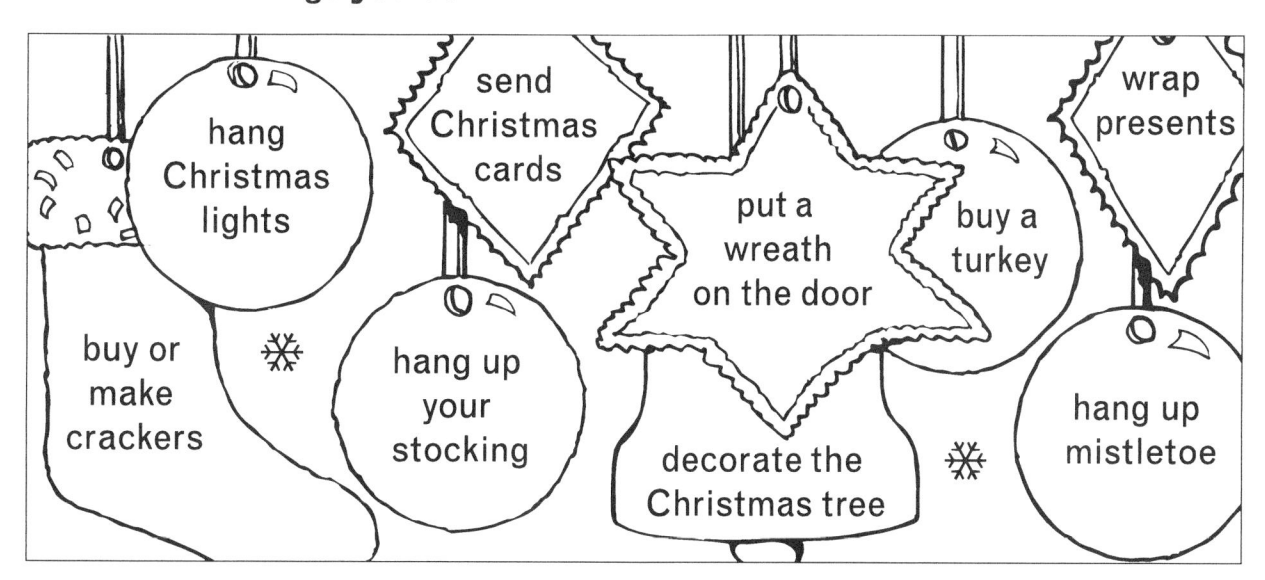

- hang Christmas lights
- send Christmas cards
- put a wreath on the door
- buy a turkey
- wrap presents
- buy or make crackers
- hang up your stocking
- decorate the Christmas tree
- hang up mistletoe

2. In the presents, write three things you do on Christmas Day.

3. After Christmas Day, there can be a lot of rubbish. Colour the things, which could be used again next year.

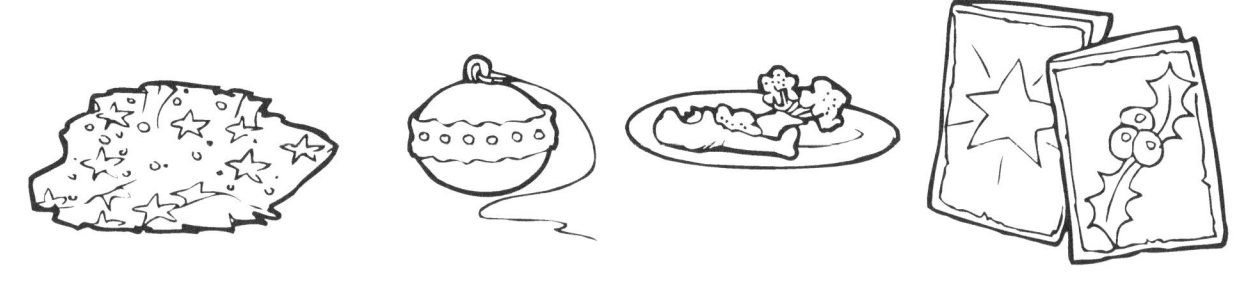

wrapping paper   decorations   leftover food   Christmas cards

Sort Santa's Sack

Learning Objectives
- Reads and classifies Christmas words.

Materials
- Copymaster

Additional Activities
1. Make a 'sack' for the wall and brainstorm Christmas words to make a bank of words the pupils can use in their writing.
2. Think of other ways the words in Santa's sack could be grouped. For example, words from the Nativity story, words about the North Pole, words about what we do at home.

Answers

Christmas Food: Christmas pudding, candy cane, turkey, Christmas cake

Christmas Characters: Santa, Rudolph, elves, angel, Baby Jesus

Christmas Decorations: Christmas tree, bell, holly, lights, star

Sort Santa's Sack

Write each word from Santa's sack in its stocking.

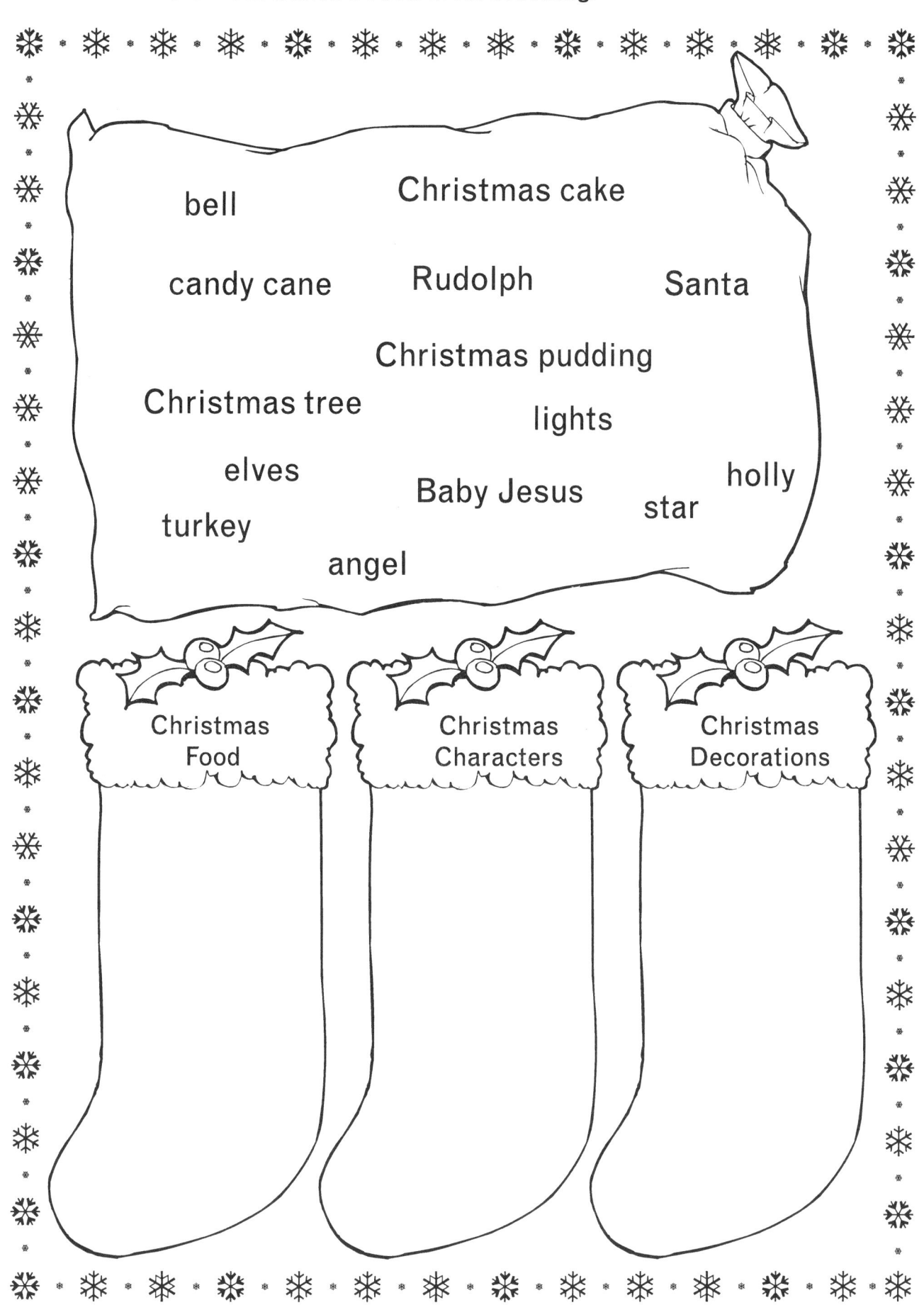

- bell
- Christmas cake
- candy cane
- Rudolph
- Santa
- Christmas pudding
- Christmas tree
- lights
- elves
- Baby Jesus
- holly
- turkey
- star
- angel

Christmas Food

Christmas Characters

Christmas Decorations

Ho! Ho! Hold on!

Learning Objectives
- Comprehends a visual text and sequences its events

Materials
- Copymaster
- Blank paper strip

Additional Activities
1. Ask the pupils to write a brief description of what is happening below the pictures they have sequenced.
2. Create a cartoon strip by adding speech bubble cut-outs and writing what the characters are saying in each picture.

Answers
1. Santa puts harnesses on his reindeer.
2. Santa gets into his sleigh.
3. A strap gets caught on a tree.
4. The reindeer are unfastened and fly away—Santa calls to them.
5. The reindeer return and are refastened.
6. Santa and his team fly away together.

Ho! Ho! Hold on!

Cut out the pictures and glue them in order.

I think we are ready to go.	Ho, Ho, Ho! Merry Christmas!
	Come back!
Let me put your harness on.	Now we won't get caught on that tree!

The Christmas Kit

Spot the Differences

Learning Objectives
- Visually discriminates and circles the differences between two pictures.

Materials
- Copymaster
- Pencils

Additional Activities
1. Use the pictures to play barrier games such as those suggested on page 16 of the *Christmas Kit*.

Answers
1. Part of trim on Santa's sleigh missing
2. Teddy has black nose
3. Present missing ribbon
4. Slipper missing fluff
5. Zip on Santa's sleeping bag
6. Ribbon on present in sleigh now spotted
7. Mountain has lost snow
8. Reindeer sled missing
9. Reindeer lost antler
10. Sack in sleigh has no top

Spot the Differences

Look at the pictures. Some things are different. Can you find them? Circle ten different things in the picture below.

The Christmas Kit

Letter to Santa

Learning Objectives
- Uses reading comprehension strategies such as reading on and sentence structure to predict missing words.
- Proofreads a text to check for meaning.

Materials
- Copymaster
- Scissors

Additional Activities
1. Pupils can write their own letter to Santa and post it in a class 'mailbox'. Class members can pretend to be Santa and respond to the letters.
2. Pupils can visit the website *http//www.santas.net* and register their wish list with Santa on-line. Pupils will also be able to find out if they have been 'naughty or nice' at this website!

Answers
1. Dear
2. hope
3. your
4. well
5. have
6. good
7. you
8. me
9. for
10. hello

Letter to Santa

Choose from the words below to finish the letter to Santa.

[____] Santa,

I [____] you and [____] reindeer are [____].

I [____] been very [____] this year and was wondering if [____] could bring [____] a new bike [____] Christmas.

Please say '[____]' to Mrs Claus for me.

Your friend,

Corey

well	have	hope	hello	me
you	Dear	good	your	for

Christmas Colouring

Learning Objectives
- Determines the attributes of a diamond (size and colour) to select the correct colours and reveal a secret picture.

Materials
- Copymaster
- Coloured pencils

Background information

The Christmas stocking originated from a story concerning the charity of St Nicholas. Legend has it that three poor sisters had left their stockings to dry by the fireplace. St Nicholas had thrown gold pieces through the smoke hole (chimneys were unknown) and these had lodged inside the stockings. The tale spread and soon many people were hanging stockings by the fire in the hope that they too might find gold pieces from St Nicholas. The fact that 25 December was dedicated to the memory of St Nicholas linked his life, his charity and the stocking with the celebration of the birth of Christ.

Additional Activities

1. Make Christmas stockings to hang in the classroom. These could be made from felt pieces and sewn or constructed simply from paper and decorated.
2. Discuss the attributes of shapes and use these attributes to classify groups of two- or three-dimensional objects.

Christmas Colouring

Follow the code to colour the shapes. You will see a mystery Christmas object!

◇ – white   ○ – yellow   ✶ – green   ● – red

Prim-Ed Publishing   www.prim-ed.com   *The Christmas Kit*   53

Santa's Christmas Clues

Learning Objectives
- Uses word attack strategies to predict words in a secret message and to construct words which may have unfamiliar spelling.

Materials
- Copymaster

Additional Activities
1. Pupils can make their own code to send secret messages to their classmates.
2. Model a rebus story using some of the pictures in the code (use pictures to replace some words in the story). Encourage the pupils to write their own story using rebus symbols.

Answers
1. I will come when you are asleep.
2. Teacher check

Santa's Christmas Clues

Santa has put together a secret message to tell you when he will visit your house!

1. **Use the code to find out when Santa will visit. Each picture in the code starts with the letter it stands for.**

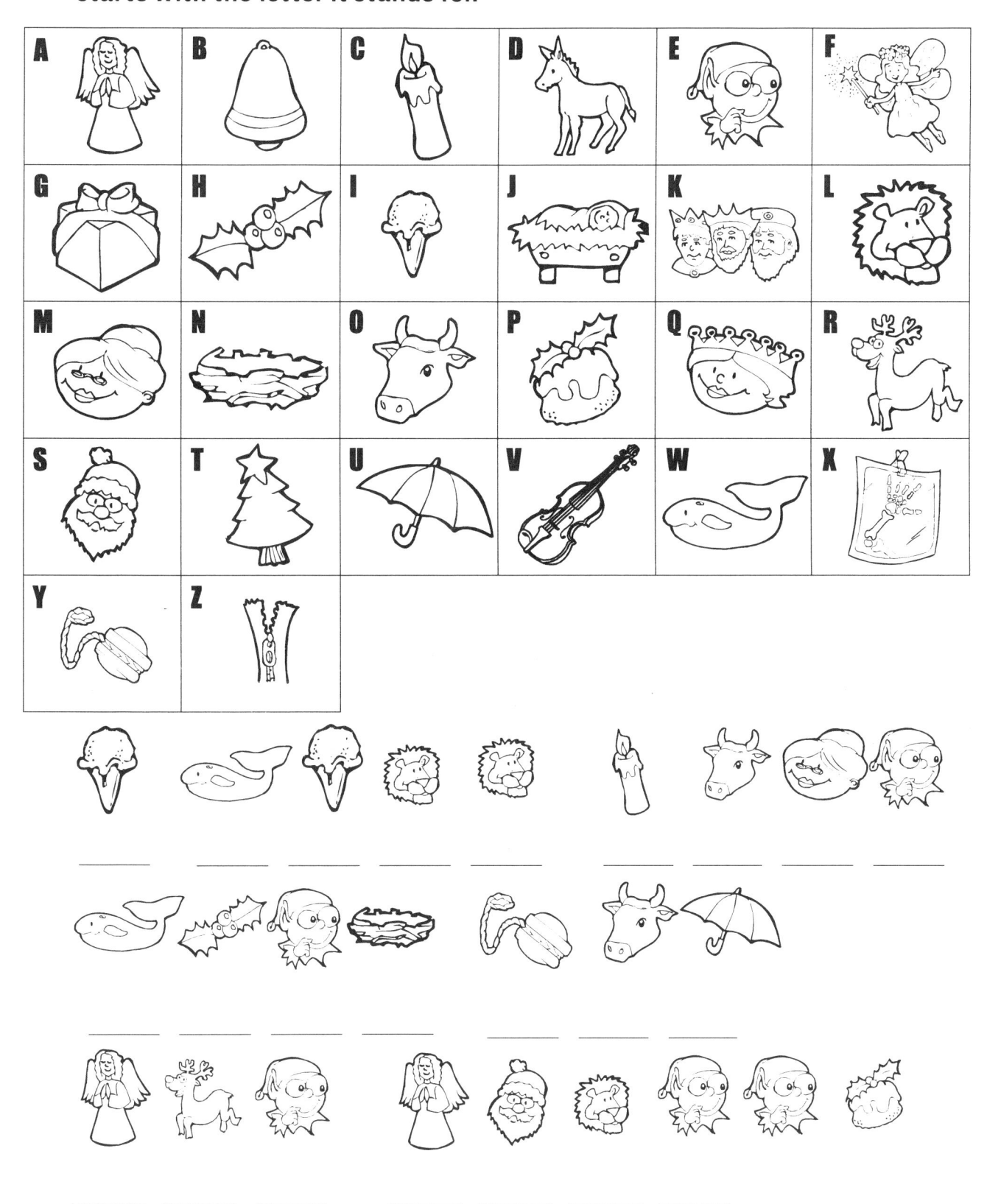

A	B	C	D	E	F
angel	bell	candle	donkey	elf	fairy

G	H	I	J	K	L
gift	holly	ice-cream	Jesus	kings	lion

M	N	O	P	Q	R
mother	nest	ox	pudding	queen	reindeer

S	T	U	V	W	X
Santa	tree	umbrella	violin	whale	x-ray

Y	Z
yo-yo	zip

_ _ _ _ _ _ _ _ _ _

_ _ _ _ _ _ _

_ _ _ _ _ _ _ _ _ _ _

2. **Use the code above to create your own Christmas sentence on the back of this sheet. Give your code to a friend to solve.**

Colour and Count

Learning Objectives

- Creates a path by counting.
- Identifies regular two-dimensional shapes.
- Counts to 31.

Materials

- Copymaster

Additional Activities

1. If the class is having a 'Secret Santa', use the presents to classify three-dimensional shapes according to their attributes.
2. Make a three-dimensional Christmas tree by cutting out three Christmas tree shapes of identical size, folding them in half and stapling or sticky taping each side to a different tree cutout.

Answers

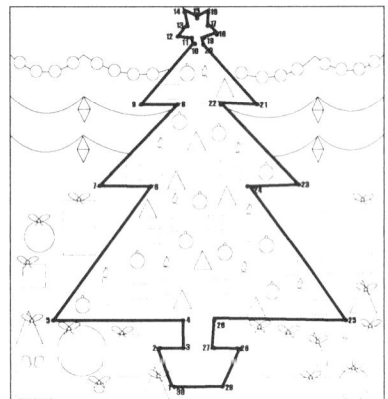

1.

2. (a) There are 31 circles.
   (b) There are 13 squares.
   (c) There are 14 rectangles.
   (d) There are 20 triangles.

Colour and Count

1. **Join the dots by following the numbers 1 – 30.**

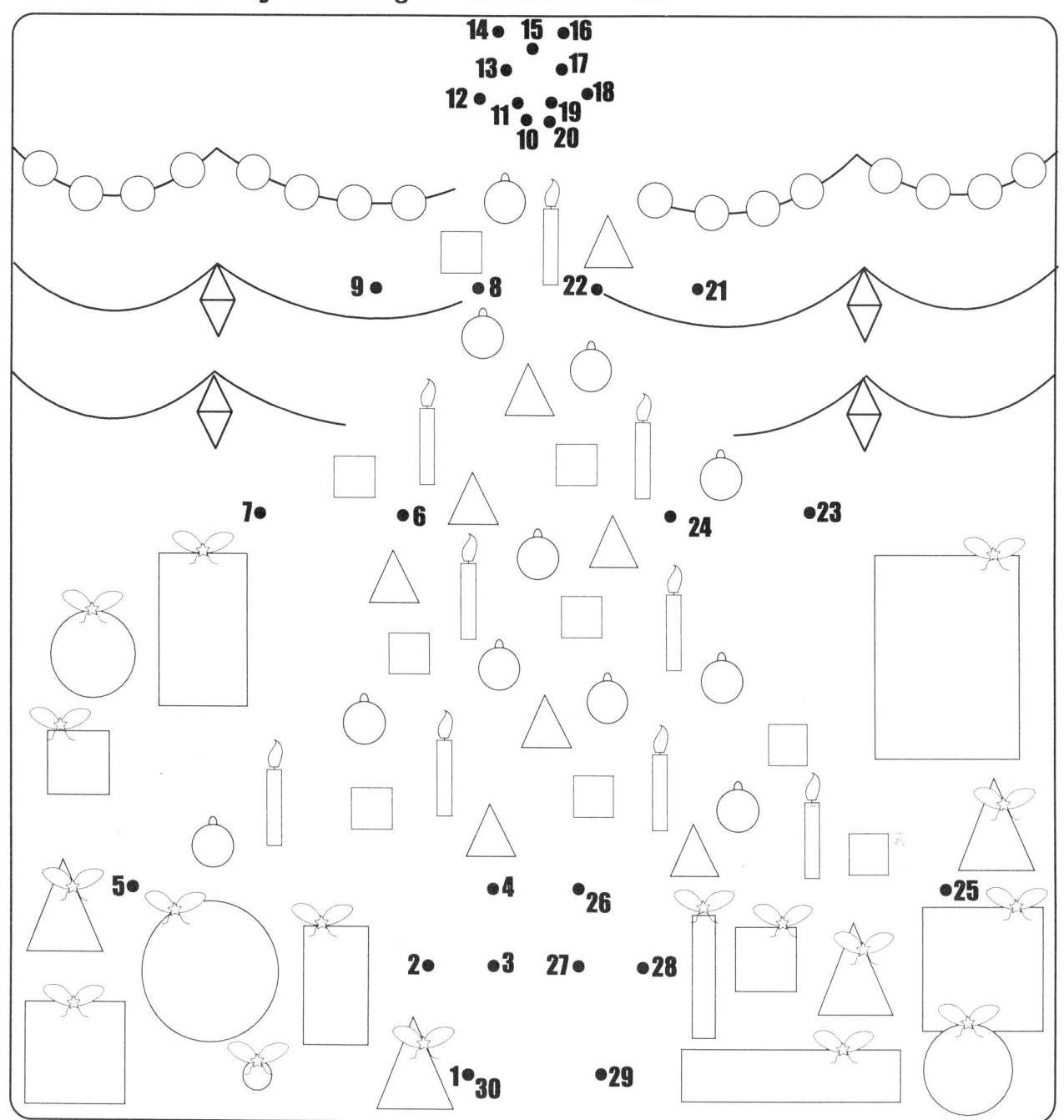

2. **Answer these questions.**

   (a) Colour the circles blue.

   There are _____ circles.

   (b) Colour the squares red.

   There are _____ squares.

   (c) Colour the rectangles yellow.

   There are _____ rectangles.

   (d) Colour the triangles orange.

   There are _____ triangles.

Rudolph's Jigsaw

Learning Objectives
- Uses spatial awareness to flip, turn and slide puzzle pieces and complete the picture.

Materials
- Copymaster
- Scissors
- Blank piece of paper

Additional Activities
1. Pupils can create their own jigsaw puzzles using pictures from old Christmas cards, their own pictures or paintings mounted on card.
2. Use tangram pieces to make common Christmas shapes such as a Christmas tree, bell, candle, star etc.

Answers

Rudolph's Jigsaw

Colour then cut out the pictures below to make Rudolph's jigsaw.

Star Magic

Learning Objectives
- Follows abstract numeric directions to complete a star.
- Uses a ruler to produce straight, accurate lines.

Materials
- Copymaster

Additional Activities
1. Pupils can create more abstract stars by placing five or six points randomly on a page and then joining each point to the remaining points.
2. To increase the difficulty of this copymaster, the pupils can be asked to cover the instructions and have a classmate give them the instructions orally, as they would in a barrier game.

Answers

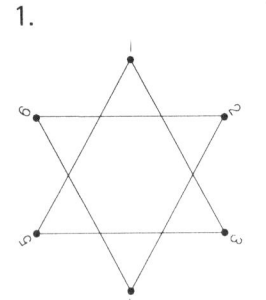

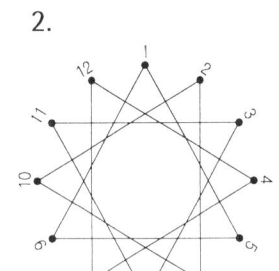

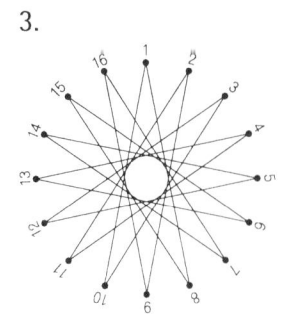

1.
2.
3.

Star Magic

1. **Use your ruler and the instructions to join the numbers and make Christmas stars.**
2. **Colour your stars using bright colours.**

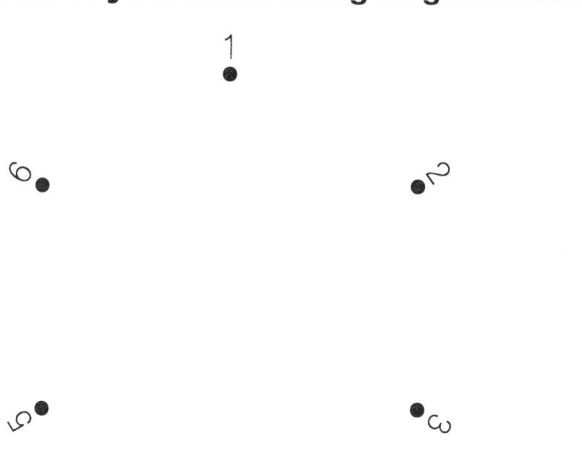

Join: 1 – 3
2 – 4
3 – 5
4 – 6
5 – 1
6 – 2

Join: 1 – 5   1 – 9
2 – 6   2 – 10
3 – 7   3 – 11
4 – 8   4 – 12
5 – 9
6 – 10
7 – 11
8 – 12

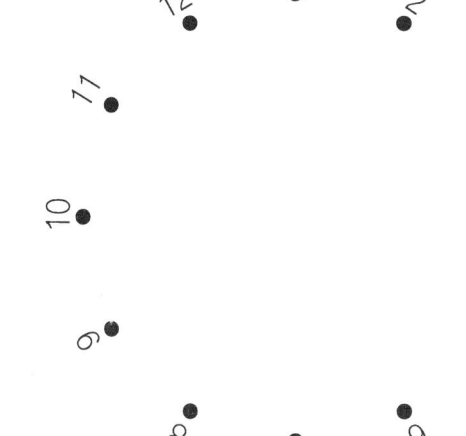

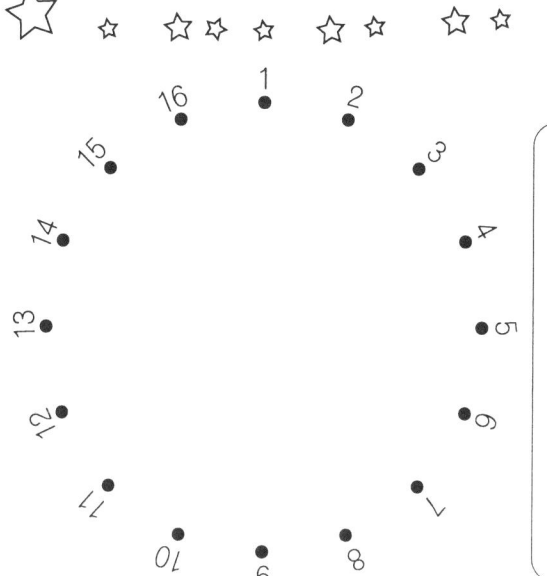

Join: 1 – 8   1 – 10
2 – 9   2 – 11
3 – 10   3 – 12
4 – 11   4 – 13
5 – 12   5 – 14
6 – 13   6 – 15
7 – 14   7 – 16
8 – 15   9 – 16

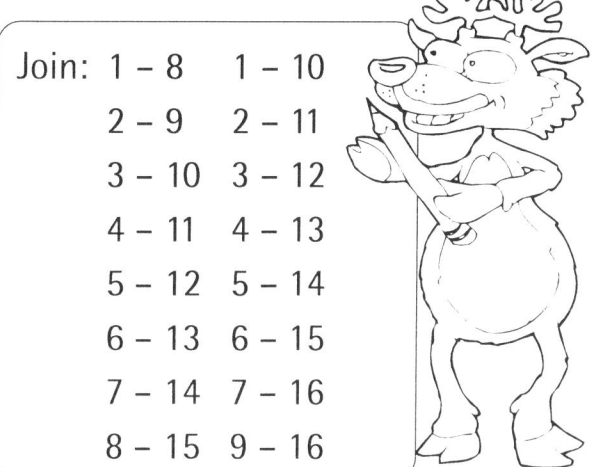